AF264379

Bringing Out the Best in Your Teenagers

*A Must-Read For Teachers, Parents,
Teenagers, and College Students*

by

Dr. Stan L. Lawton, D.Div.

5-Star Reading

Copyrights©2026

All Rights Reserved by Dr. Stan Lawton

Dedication

Dedicated to all the parents and teenagers navigating life's challenges. May you find the strength to build your own paths and the wisdom to seek guidance along the way.

About The Author

I wrote this book for parents and teenagers because I understand the struggle of navigating life without a clear map. Growing up in a dysfunctional home, I lacked a foundation of structure, discipline, and the safety of defined boundaries I had to forge those for myself. Through deliberate effort, resilience, and a steadfast "never-quit" attitude, I built my identity and purpose, anchored by the long-term intentionality required to achieve my goals.

My years of service as a police officer, firefighter, and EMT provided a high-stakes training ground that later fueled my success as both an author and a franchise owner. In those roles, I learned that life is a relentless series of decisions where the margin between triumph and tragedy, or success and failure, relies heavily on the discipline established before disaster strikes. I realized that if I could maintain that level of structure under extreme pressure, I could certainly guide teenagers with clarity, purpose, and positive reinforcement. This book is the essential guide I wish my own parents had owned.

Table of Contents

Chapter 1...1

Born for Integrity

Chapter 2..17

Born for Purpose

Chapter 3..24

Born to Share

Chapter 4..31

Born to Be the Best Possible You

Chapter 5..38

Born to Achieve

Chapter 6..52

Born with Will Power

Chapter 7..66

Born to Learn

Chapter 1
Born for Integrity

Integrity:

"The quality of being honest and having strong moral and ethical principles."

Developing a Strong Will

When you are talking about integrity, you must develop a strong will to do what is right. You may not have been brought up in a home atmosphere where your parent showed you what integrity looks like in a person. Having integrity and a strong will are among the leading principles of success in life. To be strong will mean you have the right to take up for yourself. Being a strong-willed individual does not mean being arrogant, mean, or hateful, or pushing people around. A person with integrity will have a strong foundation of conviction, which will build strong relationships.

The basic concept of integrity is honoring your word and carrying out what you said you would do. If you say you will do something, then you need to accept that responsibility. You are only as good as your word.

Being a person of integrity may take some time, depending on how you were raised and the experiences you have had. People look up to those whom they can trust. Maybe when you were little, people promised you things, but never came through. You may have had a life of broken promises because those who promised you had very little to no integrity of their own. So you may be someone who sees your disappointments as a measure of integrity.

Family Life

Some homes simply do not teach integrity, not because parents don't care, but because they are broken themselves. You may have been bounced around in a foster home where there was very little integrity demonstrated in the home. You, as a child, may have even been exposed to some kind of abuse in the home. Your dad may have appeared mad most of the time and had taken out some kind of abuse out on you or the family. Your mother or father may have had a drinking or drug problem. The family behavior in your home life may have been very dysfunctional. In your home, you never learned much about integrity. You had no choice as to what family you were born into or what country you were raised in. It may be a white family, a black family, an Asian family, a Latino family, a rich family, or a poor family you were born into. Where you were born and to what family you were born into do not determine the success you will achieve in the future.

All families have some type of dysfunction where they are dealing with bad behavior. It may have been a survival situation for you. The one thing, as a child or a teenager, that you need to understand is that it may not have been your fault. Your family environment may be a large part of your dysfunction. Even if your family environment may be a large part of your dysfunction, do not use it as a crutch or an excuse. You are better than that. You were not the cause of your family's ill behavior, but you may have absorbed some of those dysfunctional traits into your thinking as you were around adults growing up. I did to a certain point. I also had to learn to purge that kind of thinking out of my mind.

Rise Up

The key is to rise up and conquer those bad experiences that are trying to conquer you. Just remember, it is not how you start out in life, but how you finish. Don't look at all the bad circumstances in your life as a setback, but as a springboard to push you forward. The difference between being a bum all your life and being successful is in your attitude. So many teenagers are trapped by their bad attitudes. I came from a home life that was less than satisfactory. My mother was a drunk, even though she worked hard and did her best to take care of us. My mom and dad got into some fierce arguments.

I saw things at five and six years old that I should have never been a witness to. My mom, in her final years, gave up drinking. If you had taken a survey, coming from the home life I experienced, I would have been voted the least likely to succeed in life. I had no guidance or direction from my parents. I started to hang around the bums from my neighborhood and across town. I quit high school at the age of 16 for almost two years and hung out with the pot heads, the speed heads, the druggies, and the partiers. Then something happened.

One day, the thought came to me that I wanted to make something of myself. I was around 17 years of age when the thought came to me. In my life, I knew I did not want to be a failure or a bum for the rest of my life. So I made the smart move to go back to high school at the age of 18. I graduated mid-term in January when I was 20 years old. I was no doubt the oldest graduate at that time. I was not ashamed of going back to school. The odds of our home making it in life were against my brother and me, and that we would not resemble anything that looked like success in life. Growing up, we ate TV dinners, pizza, and anything else that was not very good for us. Had missed the match clothes going to school.

If I had permanently quit high school, I would not be writing today and would not have accomplished all I have. Being a little dyslexic did not help either. My learning disability made it three times harder for me to learn. O ya, when I graduated high school, I could not read a complete sentence. I will share why later. I refused to let that hold me back.

I just had to work harder to be an achiever. I tried out for the high school baseball team when I went back, and would have made the team except my age at 18 disqualified me. It took a lot of determination to finish high school. I did not have a lot of integrity in my life as a teenager. I was just going along in life. So I had to learn integrity and good life principles.

How to be an honest person, how to be dependable, how to be reliable, how to honor my word did not come easy. I had to restructure my thinking. Several of my party buddies did not make the necessary changes that I made. Some ended up dying very early in life from car accidents, some committed suicide, others ended up being drunks, and others spent a long time in jail. One of my partying buddies spent 28 years in jail for ripping people off in business. No integrity. He was not a person of excellence.

Let me list 14 basic principles about integrity.

1. Paying your bills on time.
2. Do not spend more than you have.
3. Treating people fairly.
4. Being a person of your word.
5. Stay away from drugs and those who do drugs.
6. Treat people with kindness.
7. Do not drive under the influence of alcohol.
8. Show up to work on time.
9. Be loyal.
10. Be dependable.
11. Be willing to help others.
12. Think about the consequences before making a decision.
13. Learn to balance your checkbook.
14. Finish High School.

Code of Conduct

I had to build into my life a code of conduct. Conduct is the manner in which one behaves. Code is a systematic collection of rules and regulations one lives by. So I had to develop a system that I imposed on myself for the way I wanted to live my life. It is not easy to train yourself. It was not easy coming from a dysfunctional family. I found out that people will grade you in life on your code of conduct. If you live your life in a disorderly and reckless fashion, your chances of succeeding in life will not prevail. You will always find yourself continuously in trouble. A life of regret and misery is no way to live. Let me say this: all the money in the world will not buy you integrity or good life principles, much less make you happy.

Why Rules and Regulations

You may say, I don't believe in rules and regulations. I'm going to do what I want. I am going to do life my way. A lot of my friends did just that. Most are now dead, and some ended up in jail. What a life!! They did not achieve much in life.

They were, for the most part, selfish, egotistical, self-centered individuals. Their reputation and quality of life were crap. Did they win in life? No. You may live in a bad part of your city where gangs, violence, drugs, and guns are around every corner, and neighborhood children are getting shot by drive-by shooters.

Most teenagers give up and say what the heck. I'll never get out of here. That is a lie. You can achieve being the best you can be in the most difficult situations. I found out that I did not let my home situation determine who I was going to be. I would not let my past failures determine my future successes. Growing up, I was also a type of rebel. I never listened to people who were smarter than me. I did not have any family support. I thought I knew it all. Wrong! This attitude was getting me nowhere, and I mean nowhere. I had no structure in my life, no discipline, and I knew I had to change. I went back and completed high school. One of the best moves I had ever made. Don't be left behind. Your future depends on it.

Encourage Yourself

You may not have had the needed encouragement in your home life, but don't let that stop you. Begin to encourage yourself. You will need to tell yourself that I can make it, I can do it. Do not let anyone label you as someone who can't. Do not let anyone label you as a loser. Don't buy into anyone who tells you you're a loser. When I was 14 years of age, I asked my father to come and watch me play. I was a good baseball player and still am today. I wanted him to be proud of me. In New York, our little league team was very good and won many games. We moved to South Carolina for a short spell. At 12 years old, I had the highest batting average in the league for that one year. We moved again to Virginia.

He is where it changed. At 14 & 15 years old, even though I was picked to go to Tennessee as an all-star, I was not on a winning team. My

father said I don't want to come and see you lose. Actually, I took it as he was calling me a loser. I never really bought into those words. Subconsciously, it did cause me to doubt myself, and maybe some of that caused me to quit school. For a while, I may have had low self-esteem. It took a little bit to gather myself. No one knew my future, and no one knows your future. Begin to speak positive words to yourself. Keep your head down and study hard. If you see someone else who needs help, begin to encourage them. Success and leadership are developed from within you.

Trust me when I say this. You may have to break off some friendships and relationships that are not good for you, as I did. My so-called friends were not pushing me in the right direction, and they did not have my best interests in mind. I had to separate myself from them in my life as a teenager. The truth is, after all the fun and partying days are over, they will not be there for you. Choose your friend carefully.

No one had to tell me I needed to finish high school. I surely did not get the encouragement to stay in school from my parents or my so-called friends. I had a built-in determination. There were times, as I was finally growing up, when I would still make mistakes, and I still did not do everything exactly right. It took time to change my behavior.

I began to reflect and learn from them. Sometimes I had to learn the lesson the hard way. This does take time to get it right. I had to put restraints on myself. It was not easy, so don't kick yourself if you don't do things exactly right. It will happen to you. Get back up and keep pressing forward.

The Easy Way Out

You will learn that taking the easy way out or shortcutting your education will only damage you and your chances to move ahead. You have to learn not to compromise your integrity. Let me say, lying, cheating, and stealing will only come back to haunt you and destroy your life. There is a universal principle that is alive and well. How a person treats others, he or she will be treated. Most people are not familiar with this universal law. When you treat someone else rudely or disrespectfully, you yourself will be treated rudely and disrespectfully. When you steal from someone, you yourself will suffer a great loss. When you do drugs, death is around the corner.

When we consider others before we consider ourselves, we take the high road in life. What you give in life will be returned to you. Your life is like a farmer always planting seeds. If you plant bad behavior, it will come back with very bad results. For many young people, bad decisions are called jail time. I talked about this guy in the neighborhood where I grew up. He was a swindler and a cheat. His behavior was horrible, and he thought he could get over on customers. That got him 28 years in prison. His brother served time as well as his partner.

The two brothers were in a good and profitable business. But when they began to mistreat customers, lie, and take advantage of the elderly, it caught up with them. Their bad and corrupted behavior caught up with them and destroyed their lives. If they had conducted themselves with integrity, honesty, and run their business above board, they would have been well respected and appreciated. They were greedy and could not wait to be rich. When they shortcut the system and try to take the easy way out, they lose.

Remember, success takes honesty and integrity. Success is built over time and is not a sprint, but a marathon. Taking the easy way is not always the right thing to do. It has many drawbacks. In college, when I would write a paper and turn it in, I did the necessary research because I wanted to learn. I did not want to just get by. I did not have to go to all that extra effort. I could have written something nice and gotten a good grade.

Because I made the additional effort, I ran up on some information that is very vital to me today. You will be surprised by what you can learn that stays with you when you put in the extra work.

Identify

A person needs to identify what is poor and unacceptable behavior. In today's world, people are so mixed up. Some students have no idea what the difference is between right and wrong. We know that lying, being dishonest, cheating, stealing, and taking advantage of people is wrong behavior. To stay in the realm of wrong behavior makes a person inferior, a second - class individual with questionable motives.

There is a way in life that may seem right to a person, but the underlying results will lead them to tragedy. Look at all the athletes who have made wrong decisions, and it ended their careers. They ended up broke, and some were homeless.

You go to a party or hang out with friends to have fun, and there are drugs offered to you. You have no idea what the drug has been laced with. Now the simple drugs turn into the deadliest thing you could put in your mouth. Do you trust your friend? Do you now trust the dealer? The answer to both those questions is that you do not trust any street drug or a friend who is doing drugs. Your future depends on making the right choices. Again, your future depends on making the right choices. Walking away from possible trouble and those who have questionable behavior is the greatest move anyone can make. Walking away from those situations that can hurt your future makes you a stronger individual and a leader people can follow.

Little Things Do Matter

Sometimes it isn't the big things in life, it is the little things. The little things we overlook that can spoil and damage our lives. This must sound a little crazy. Showing integrity is as simple as picking up a piece of paper off the floor and putting it into the trash can. You might say, "I did not put it there," and, "Why should I pick it up?" Think how many people have walked by that piece of paper and never considered picking it up. Just ordinary people never think to take the simple steps to help.

What does it matter if no one picks the piece of paper up? It can show that people are not willing to go out of their way to help. It seems insignificant, but it is not. There is no glory in picking the paper up and discarding it.

The person who picks up the piece of paper and puts it into the trash is setting the example for others to follow by their actions. Doing what it takes when others will not begins to shape our leadership skills. That is what integrity is about. Having integrity produces good behavior. Good behavior produces integrity.

Opening a door for someone who passes in front of you is being very considerate. Helping the elderly and those who are less fortunate in life shows kindness. In the long run, it is the little things in life that will make the difference. Good leaders will have a strong, excellent attitude. Think about it. Seemingly, picking up a piece of paper and placing it in the trash can does not mean you have to clean up your street. Putting grocery items back where they belong is an example for others to follow. People are always watching. Another small principle about integrity is cleaning up after yourself. You make the mess; you clean it up. No one has the responsibility to clean up after you. Don't live like a slob. Dress well. It is the little things you do that people see, which they examine in your life.

It's a Matter of Choice

To live a life of integrity is a matter of choice. It is not forced on anybody, but it is an option. Integrity will make you rise above the crowd, and people will take notice. If people took a survey, how would they describe you? Thoughtful, kind, encouraging, reassuring, insightful, or would they say you are unsupportive, discouraging, selfish, self-centered, greedy, wasteful, and not sensitive toward others? Only you can make up the rules for your life on how some people may see you. I understand that not everyone will see you in the same way or see your potential. That does not matter, you run your life's race.

There has to be some good quality in you that people can relate to. Our purpose in life is also found in the quality of our living. Sometimes our bad qualities will overshadow any good qualities we may have. Bad qualities are what we call our weaknesses. The weaknesses you may have can be turned into strengths. If you are a procrastinator by nature, you have to set yourself a goal to learn to do things right away. Don't wait until later. Procrastination is not a desirable habit in your life. You always said, I will do it later and sometimes later never comes. You want to build good habits through repetition. Procrastination generally forms negative impressions, associating the person with undesirable traits, potential unreliability, and a lack of motivation.

Dealing with Issues

In my career as a police officer, firefighter, and EMT, I had the opportunity to work under many supervisors. For the most part, I got along well with all the lieutenants and captains. However, there was one fire department captain who was particularly difficult to work under. He had a complex personality; he was overly stern and seemingly displayed an uncaring attitude towards those who worked beneath him. The environment became so challenging that, at one point, the entire team of ten firefighters at Station #1 felt compelled to file a formal complaint against him with the chief.

I don't know how that situation ultimately resolved, but it was clear that his inability to treat people with respect overshadowed any positive qualities he may have had. While I recognize he possessed some strengths, his weaknesses prevailed, leaving me with mixed feelings about him as a person. He often acted as if he was above others until he was caught driving under the influence of alcohol, resulting in a conviction that, surprisingly, did not cost him his job. Life has a way of humbling us, and I remember him for that lesson. Now, I understand he is suffering from dementia, which raises my concern for his welfare.

Reflecting on my experiences, I realize that when faced with difficult decisions, it is crucial not to act impulsively. Engaging in conversation with someone can provide valuable perspective and help clarify your thoughts. I experienced this firsthand while working under that challenging captain. The pressure was immense, and I nearly decided to leave the fire department. However, I sought advice from Assistant Fire Chief Bob Anderson, who offered insights that profoundly changed my perspective and encouraged me to stay. His guidance proved to be one of the best professional decisions I made, especially when, shortly thereafter, the captain was transferred to headquarters.

This experience reaffirmed the importance of seeking counsel before making significant decisions. It also highlights that everyone has character flaws, and it takes time and effort to address them. Your strength lies in your good qualities, but you must also work on your shortcomings. People need to see your integrity in life, and it is through your positive attributes that you will shine. Here is a list of some common character flaws that can hinder integrity; see if you can relate to any of these. It takes a strong person to confront their character flaws, and doing so is essential for personal and professional growth.

1. Egotistical or self-righteous.

2. Vain or thinking of being superior.

3. Lascivious or having excessive desire to control.

4. Predatory or seeking to exploit.

5. Excessive pride or one who is not teachable.

6. Deluded or easily deceived.

7. A boastful person or one who likes to brag.

8. A person without understanding is always being critical of and finding fault in others.

These are some of the character flaws we want to stay away from. When a person decides they want to be the best possible person that they can be, they must take an inventory of their conduct and behavior. We all have character flaws. I like to call them weaknesses. This is all a part of our training to build our integrity in life. We all need to rise up in our conduct. The more you understand, the fewer mistakes you will make in life. When it comes to our integrity, discipline must be a reality in your life. It is as simple as making your bed in the morning. Washing and putting up the dishes. Keeping your space clean and tidy.

When you look at martial arts, you see it as training in self-defense. It is much more. In the adult classes I attended at the time, they were after the children's class. I watched the instructor as he handled the children and corrected their form so they properly demonstrated the technique. Repetition brings results.

As the children started their classes, the instructor told them to put their shoes against the wall neatly. They started off with warm-ups. At the end of the class, the instructor told them to make sure they listened to their partner. The students looked up to the instructor. Then he said, "Do you understand?"

Their response was, "Yes, sir." The military is the same, it is called boot camp. A good leader wants to prepare you and train you to face life's most difficult situations. So many teenagers today are not prepared to take on what we call life. So my call to you is, "Are you ready to have a life of integrity?"

Chapter 2
Born for Purpose

Have you ever asked yourself why I am here? What is my purpose in life? So many people ask that question every day. Many people become increasingly unfulfilled as they grow older. One thing we all have inside of us is the ability to accomplish anything we put our minds to. Sometimes our purpose in life is revealed in our childhood. Every person since man has been present on the earth has been born with some type of talent, ability, or desire to accomplish something meaningful in their life. Man has always had a creative ability inside them. I look at the pyramids in Egypt and wonder, how did they accomplish that enormous task? The engineering was incredible. They had a tremendous creative ability. Around 2780 BCE, King Djoser's architect, Imhotep, built the first pyramid.

What about math? The development of mathematics did not exist until around 3000 BC. The ancient Sumerians of Mesopotamia developed a complex system of metrology from 3000 BC. From 2600 BC onwards, the Sumerians wrote multiplication tables on clay tablets and dealt with geometrical exercises and division problems.

https://www.google.com/search?q=sumerians+civilization+in+mathmatics&rlz.

The classical Greek period, from 600 to 300 B.C., used mathematics as an expanding discipline. From the beginning of mathematics, we now have several disciplines such as geometry, algebra, calculus, just to name a few. I believe that the universe was created through the art of mathematics. This concept is known as the Mathematical Universe Hypothesis.

In China, history records the many contributions now known as the Chinese experience. It was the development of mechanics, hydraulics, and mathematics applied to horology (the study and measurement of time) metallurgy, metallurgy (the branch of science and technology concerned with the properties of metals and their production and purification), astronomy, agriculture, engineering, music theory, craftsmanship, naval architecture, and warfare.

The use of the plow during the Neolithic period, Longshan culture (c. 3000–c 2000 BC) allowed for high agricultural production yields and the rise of Chinese civilization during the Shang Dynasty (1600–c 1050 BC). Later inventions, such as the multiple-tube seed drill and the heavy moldboard iron plow, enabled China to sustain a much larger population through improvements in agricultural inventions.

https://en.wikipedia.org/wiki/List_of_Chinese_inventions

The first modern electronic digital computer was called the Atanasoff–Berry computer, or ABC. It was built by physics Professor John Vincent Atanasoff and his graduate student, Clifford Berry, in 1942 at Iowa State College, known as Iowa State University. https://theconversation.com/what-was-the-first-computer-12216

Every person, no matter what their position, purpose, talent, ability, or desire in life is, is extremely important towards building a successful community, which will lead to the success of a nation. It is the domino effect. It might seem like some positions are more important than others. In reality, it is not true. Just because a person may make more money in a position does not diminish the importance of someone else's position.

A CEO of a company may have more responsibility in their position and make more money, but what would happen if the sanitation workers went on strike for four weeks? Let the firefighters, police officers, or nurses go on strike. What about the railroad worker or the truck driver going on strike? Whose job is more important now? See how a community needs everyone to work together.

We all thought Thomas Edison was the inventor of the light bulb. It was actually Humphry Davy. In 1802, Humphry Davy invented the first electric light. He experimented with electricity and invented an electric battery. When he connected wires to his battery and a piece of carbon, the carbon glowed, producing light. His invention was known as the Electric

Arc lamp. And while it produced light, it didn't produce a long glow and was much too bright for practical use. Over the next seven decades, other inventors also created "light bulbs," but no designs emerged for commercial application. https://www.bulbs.com/learning/history.aspx.

Humphry Davy was much like the Wright brothers, who successfully flew a machine that could fly and were America's aviation pioneers. Like Humphry Davy, they were the pioneers of their industry. Many other patents were filed, but no one could successfully create the light bulb for commercial use. The patents were sold to Thomas Edison. In 1880, Thomas Edison's company, Edison Electric Light Company, began marketing its new product. Humphry Davy could only take his invention so far.

Thomas Edison's work expanded on the creation of the light bulb that Humphry pioneered. There have been many inventions that others have modified or even redesigned, which have become useful items. Look at the different designs just from the light bulb. We now have LED lights that can light up a room. Consider the old model cars, the modern cars, and the technology inside the automobiles today. Just think what life will be like in 20 to 30 years with the advancement of technology.

The building of the Empire State Building in New York City is a beautiful sight that took the effort of many people to accomplish the task. No one person had the ability to accomplish its completion on their own. It took thousands of people with different professional talents and abilities to finish the project. Because people pulled together, we today have the privilege to see the finished product. The purpose for your life may not be revealed yet. As you grow older, a desire may begin to form in your thinking on what your purpose in your life is. It may be a trade profession, such as a plumber, electrician, welder, or carpenter. Most businesses are service-oriented. When it comes to purpose, it may take several different forms, but one outcome. Let me explain.

I had a desire when I was young to be either a forest ranger, a police officer, or a firefighter. Each of those professions was different in its job duties, but they all had one thing in common. It was public service. So in my life, I became a professional police officer, firefighter, and EMT. So my life was designed to be in public service. I did want to play professional baseball. Well. As I have gotten older, the desire to write has been added to my life. My mom was a waitress, and my dad was a custodian at a high school. These positions were both in public service. Helping others. My brother was a manager of a well-known restaurant chain for 26 years. Now he is a pastor of a community church. Our family was destined to be in public service. All professions are needed to make everything work.

After my retirement from the city, I purchased a franchise that continued my public service. Even though I had several jobs in different professions, they were all important to the community. The foot cannot say to the hand I don't need you, any more than the president of the United States can say to the border patrol or to the firefighter or police officer on the street I have no need of you. The restaurant owner cannot say to the dishwasher or to the waitress I have no need of you. The physicians cannot say to the nurses I do not need you. Everyone has a purpose. Every job is important. Everyone is needed.

If you're in high school or beginning your studies in college, what do you think your purpose in life is? The decisions you make in high school are the beginning of your journey throughout this life. Every step in school is your training ground. Learning math, English, history, and civics may not seem to be important to you right now, but they create the foundation that you will take throughout your life. For me, I did not take high school seriously. I quit high school for about a year and a half, and then I went back. Something clicked inside me to go back. I realized the direction I was heading in was empty and destructive. My desire to be a police officer and firefighter would have never been accomplished if I quit high school for good. I would have missed out on a lot of experiences and training that would have prepared me for the next step up and promotion in life.

I would have missed being on the beginning team of the police ERT unit for our department, or what they call S.W.A.T. today, which was the Emergency Response Tactical Unit. I liked and enjoyed that position for three years.

Home Work Again

I always thought homework was a terrible burden for any student to endure. What, homework again? The teachers must hate us. That is what I thought. It may be what you think. I did not have the right concept of homework. I thought homework was to punish the students. At least I felt that way, far from it. Homework is a tool designed to build learning and to bring discipline into a student's life. In life, you're going to have to face unexpected situations that pop up from time to time. Like homework, it will give you the needed discipline to conquer situations you face. It is a discipline that you would need for college or for a job. What about math?

How does that figure into life? Glad you asked. I did not realize that mathematics was designed to help you tackle problems and come up with a correct answer. It teaches you discipline and helps you to think about past life problems.

If your mind is not trained to figure out problems and issues that you will be presented with in your life, then how are you going to get through some of the most difficult moments you will face? School has some of the basic foundational building blocks you will need. Take total advantage of the time. Inside of you there may be a musician, a writer, a police officer, a firefighter, a senator, a president of a major corporation, or a community business leader. Only you, with diligent study, can bring out the great potential that lies inside you.

Chapter 3

Born to Share

The one thing that I have found out is that there are people who are less fortunate than we are. To be a great individual, a person must see a need to help others. We tend to judge people by their social status and view those who are down and out as not worthy of our time. We all know that there are con artists everywhere, and some are out on the street. I also know that there are great organizations designed to help individuals and families who are less fortunate. The key to being a great individual is never to look down on less fortunate people. We don't know their story.

When a child begins to understand a little about the world and becomes self-conscious, everything is his or hers, and they don't want to share. We see that in small children. We have all heard the saying "that's mine, that's mine, I want this, and I want that." So we, as good parents, teach our children to share. From a parent's point of view, it's a tug-of-war mentality with a three-year-old. Learning to share is a learned behavior. Some children are more prone to sharing than others. The ultimate goal for a parent is to break the selfish streak in our children. Nobody wants to be around selfish people.

We need to learn how to share. To share or to give is a privilege and not a burden. I like to watch different topics on YouTube. I was watching a topic on how people who are rude and ill-mannered behave in different public places. There was this mother with a three-year-old child in the store. The child was pulling items from the shelf and hitting the floor. The mother never corrected the child. Of course, the mom was asked to leave the store because of the three-year-old's bad behavior. There was an argument that ensued. As the argument continued, foul language was coming out of the mother's mouth with the child next to her. All of a sudden, the child started talking and threw out the "F" bomb. A three-year-old using the "F" bomb is totally unacceptable and should never be tolerated.

Why do I relate this story? What chance did this child have of having a successful life? I saw prison time in this child's future. Children will learn either good or bad behavior from their parents. If there is no proper training in the home, a child will have no respect for authority. This attitude will carry over into adulthood. I remember when my son was in school, a friend of his forgot his lunch. I guess my son was about eight years old or so. He did not hesitate one bit and shared his lunch with him.

That really touched my heart. We taught him to share. The rest was up to him on how he did it.

We don't share to get any recognition. We share because it is the right thing to do. It does not mean you need to go out and sell your house to get the money to share. Sharing is called caring and being a blessing. Some call it paying it forward. If someone does something kind to you, the next opportunity you have, share the kindness with someone else.

It is as simple as buying someone a cup of coffee or their lunch. In giving, never let a person know who you are. You are in it for the self-gratitude, not for the applause. A person who shares reveals something about their character. What would that be? It's not all about them. For the most part, why do people want to become a teacher, a firefighter, a nurse, a police officer, or join the military that puts them in harm's way? It is definitely not for the money. They want to share in protecting others. They want their life to mean something.

I can tell you, it is satisfying when you pull up to a scene when you pull a 300 lbs+ drunk that laying on the railroad tracks when a train is barreling down with only seconds to spare or pull a heart attack victim out of a car with no pulse and bring him back or hold the hand of an eight-year-old boy who just died in a car crash so he may not be alone.

What about trying to talk down a boyfriend with a knife to the neck of his girlfriend, or fighting with a husband who just killed his wife, while his five-year-old watched. Sharing is caring. I can tell you story after story of my life as a police officer/firefighter. Having the ability to share is a privilege. The older I get, the more important it is to help others. We live in a society that is filled with selfishness and arrogant people coming and going. Work, work, work. I have to go here, and I have to go there. I don't have time, I have to meet this deadline. We wall ourselves in with all this running. You were born to take time to share.

You were born to be a blessing. Share time with your family. Share time with your friends. Share time with your spouse and children, and even share a moment with people you don't even know. The most powerful words you can share with someone are the words "I Love You." The second most powerful words are "How Can I Help". When you share, you tell the people around you that you are not alone. Sharing can break the loneliness in someone's heart. It can bring a little cheer to someone who is discouraged. To be discouraged means the absence of courage. Courage in a person has been dismissed. You can help bring back a little courage to people by sharing a good word or doing a good deed. Again, I am not talking about someone who does not want to take care of themselves.

Our lives should demonstrate good qualities. Our life is not an island unto itself. We need to be a difference maker so others can see the good in people. By sharing your help, you bring back faith in humanity as you develop an attitude of giving and compassion.

Sharing is an investment in someone else's life. You can not put a price on that. There is no higher quality than investing in someone else. Sharing also brings people of all cultures together. Be a part of a winning attitude and begin to share. Start small, and as you grow financially, you can give a little more. At times, make yourself available to help others in need.

The benefit will be returned back to you in many ways. A study by psychologists found that stingy people have higher levels of the stress hormone cortisol. Being a stingy type of person is a lose-lose situation; I have seen firsthand that many people in poverty have an attitude of not being a giver. This attitude is more of a survival mentality. This is somewhat of a learned behavior due to their environment. Sharing is a learned behavior as well.

How do you break the vicious poverty cycle? First, you have to look at things differently. Poverty is harmful to your success in life. By learning to give in small amounts, you begin to break the poverty cycle in your life. Giving has to be voluntary because you want to come from the heart to mean something. If you give with the motivation of getting, it is somewhat selfish. There has to be no strings attached in your giving. It will not break you to leave an extra dollar when you tip your waitress or waiter, or donate that $10 to a church or to a charity that is reaching out into the community. Giving has also been linked to the release of oxytocin, which induces the feeling of warmth, euphoria, and a connection to others. This chemical reaction, when constantly repeated, improves well-being and life satisfaction and is also linked to the reduction of depression.https://www.elitedaily.com/life/join-fight-stinginess-many-benefits-generosity/770923

Sharing and giving are positive acts. I am going to tell you this story only to let you know that sharing is caring. Some years back, I was at a local restaurant in my hometown, eating lunch. It was around Christmas time. I heard two waitresses talking and how one of the young waitresses had her children's gifts for Christmas stolen. My ears began to perk up. I wasn't trying to eavesdrop, but I could still hear the conversation. The one who was sharing her unhappy event said I don't know what I am going to do. She told my waitress that the children's gifts were stolen from her car. It was very close to Christmas, and I remembered my mother being a waitress. I knew she did not have a lot of money or time to make up the difference.

My hearing her conversation was not a matter of coincidence. I did not know at the time why I was there. The waitresses did not know I was overhearing their conversation. I was just eating away. Being a dad, it hit me pretty hard. True, I can't help everyone.

That day, it was in my power to help in some small way. When I got my check, I rose from the table and left a larger-than-normal tip on the table. I am not going to tell you how much. Giving is up to you. I knew it would put a smile on her face and maybe ease the pressure she was under. What would you have done in that situation if it were in your power to help? The waitress never knew my name. I got up, paid the bill, and walked out of the restaurant. That was years ago. It does not have to be Christmas for you to help someone in need.

I was not raised rich by any means. In school, I had a lunch ticket for those kids who could not afford a lunch meal. I can tell you today, giving and sharing got me out of poverty. I am so glad I can help people. A lot of very successful people today are philanthropists. In some small way, as you share, you become a philanthropist. Become a philanthropist and seek to promote the welfare of others through giving. We should never judge the less fortunate and how they got there, because if we did, no one would share any kindness towards others. In this world, there will be people who need looking after. That is just the way it is. We need to be a person who seeks to promote the welfare of others and not discourage them. Start as a small philanthropist, and maybe, just maybe, you will become a well-known philanthropist.

Chapter 4

Born to Be the Best Possible You

There are people with the attitude to just get by. They do the minimum amount of work just to keep their job. I know that the cell phones of today have been a major distraction when it comes to work performance. I constantly see people at their workplace with their phones beside them, glancing at them every time they get a chance. The addiction is incredibly high.

In people, the attitude will be the determining factor in how successful you will become. Attitude determines altitude, in how far you will go in life. When we talk about quality of life, we are talking about your physical health, your social life, your financial life, your emotional health, your psychological health, and your spiritual life. One will always have an effect on the other. There are people who go to work so tired they can hardly keep their eyes open because they did not get the needed rest. If you're not going to take care of yourself, who will? We only get one chance in this life to be the best we can be at what we do.

Excellence

Excellence is a quality that people really appreciate, because it's so hard to find. When we talk about excellence in a person, we are talking about being extremely good at what you do. This is where your education is vital to your future. High school sets the foundation for your future. When I went back to school after a year and a half of quitting, I realized that my future was in my hands to succeed or to fail in life. I knew I had a desire or a calling in my life. So I started college.

I had a long way to go to get where I wanted to be, but I was determined to move forward. It was going to take an attitude of excellence and determination to finish. I was working at the time, so I had to take the courses as time would allow me to. I finished my Bachelor's degree, then my Master's, and then my Doctorate. It took me 16 years from start to finish. In 2000, I completed my Doctorate. I was 40 years old when that took place. I had many opportunities to quit. I did not take that door. It was very difficult at times. When you set your mind to do something, you need to see it through to completion. You will have opportunities to quit and fail, but don't take them.

Wishing

There are people who wish to accomplish good things in their lives. Wishing it to happen is just that, wishing. There is no power in wishing. You may wish for peace in the world. Until someone comes up with a good working strategy and everyone pulls together and thinks alike, it will never happen. Wishing will not bring you the needed education and training you need. It takes a step forward called effort or application. So if you want to be an architect, then begin to take classes in school. If you want to be a manager/supervisor of a corporation, then prepare and take the classes that deal with business administration. If you want to be a CPA, then go to a financial class. If you want to be a nurse, then apply to nursing school. What I am telling you is that success just does not fall out of the sky by wishing for it to happen.

Learn

You say, I don't know if I can do it? All things are possible to you if you believe in yourself. You may have been brought up always hearing that you are nothing, you won't amount to much. You're a loser. Let me say those comments are nothing but lies. I was called a loser when I was 14 years old. I refuse to believe it. I did not get the needed direction from my parents as some kids did. I had to figure it out on my own. That's Ok. Determine what your strengths are and what your weaknesses are. In me, motivation was a strength. Since I was raised somewhat on my own, I had some street smarts. I recognized I have the gift to sell. I had learned selling techniques, and I learned I had a gift for administration. Through the years, I attended leadership classes.

I learned to do paperwork and write reports. In my last job, I was dealing with around a $700,00.00 budget. I learned to schedule personnel, I learned to hire employees, and manage an office up to 10 full-time and part-time employees. I learned how to take care of complaints and deal with the public. I learned to get the financial reports ready to take to the CPA, how to order products, and about payroll. The main theme of all that is the word LEARN. I learned how to do these things. It took me over 35 years to receive all the training to equip me for the next levels in my life. You never finish where you start out. Life, it is one big learning experience. Every situation prepared me for the next challenge in life. Sometimes you have to make the hard decisions. In time, you will learn how to make the right and tough decision.

Fear

I was not going to let others determine my life's course. Negative people don't sign your paycheck. I did not operate in fear. Fear will always hold you back, but I did operate cautiously. Never jump from job to job unless you are trying to better yourself. Let me say this to you. Do not let money be your guiding light or make up your decision. Money alone has too many pitfalls. Look at the job, not the money. I knew people who jumped from a secure job because of the increase in pay and regretted it.

They tried to go back, but that bridge was burned. Not every opportunity appears to be what it seems to be. Do your homework. Everybody can put their best foot forward for a time.

Do Not Compromise

Never compromise good values. It is better to make less money than take a job with an increase in pay, and the stress of that job becomes overwhelming. Never cheat to get ahead. Cheating will eventually catch up to you. There is no price you can pay for your health. One of the keys to bringing out the best potential in you is to be a good listener and be quick to learn. A person who wants to be the best will give their full attention to a speaker during a lecture. That person will take notes and go back and meditate on the lecture. You may need to limit yourself from outside influences. Your high school or college buddies will not be with you on your journey through life.

Always study the points that apply to you that will help you grow in knowledge. Knowledge is strength. Making eye contact with the speaker or professor lets them know you are willing to learn. This expression is an open invitation in your body language that you want to learn. For instance, leaning back slumped down in your chair gives off the wrong vibes.

For instance, you may want to learn forward in the speaker's direction, absorbing the information. Look interested. Take notes. Let the speaker or professor teach you. I did this in many seminars I attended. It works. Those who are giving out the information will see this attitude in you. Great people will have a genuine interest in learning. Even now, I still pick up good pointers from a speaker to constantly improve my understanding.

See, I don't know it all. You must have a basic eagerness to learn. You don't have to push these types of people. They want to better themselves. Have you ever heard of the saying that a person is a square? It is an older statement that young people use to make. It is supposed to be a derogatory statement. A person who was called square did not always fit in. When you think about a square being equal on all sides, it tells me that a square has balance. There is no compromise in a square.

A Balanced Life

If you want to have good success, you will have to learn how to balance your work life and your personal or family life. This is so important. Why? Something always suffers if you're out of balance. When a person has been in a job for a long time, they may become mentally exhausted from the job and suffer what we call burnout. Burnout is a condition that results from being under too much stress for too long a period of time. Burnout is a state of physical, emotional, and mental exhaustion caused by prolonged or chronic stress that has not been successfully managed.

College students cramming for a test can suffer from burnout from long hours of study and very little sleep. The effect is that they cannot absorb any more information. A doctor who works 60 to 70 plus hours a week during their internship can begin to suffer from burnout before their career begins. No one person is immune to burnout. Burnout sets in over a period of time. It is chronic, not acute. So a person needs to learn how to balance their life. Have you heard the saying "no rest for the weary"? That is a lie. It is not about a flop til you drop lifestyle. You have to take the time to deprogram and rest. You may have to reprogram your priorities. It is called R&R. Rest and relaxation. You need to have some type of personal activity. Exercise is a good stress relief that your body needs. You don't have to train for the Mr. Olympia contest to relieve a stress-filled life. Swimming is another exercise you can do. Just taking a long walk can relieve stress. Burnout also affects your emotional health and work performance as well. You need downtime to regain your physical and mental strength. Taking time for yourself is a good thing. When you become a leader, you yourself will understand the importance of a healthy, balanced lifestyle.

Chapter 5

Born to Achieve

Achievement:

"To Do Things Successfully, Success is Not All About Money"

In most people's hearts, they do not want to fail. When people talk about being an achiever, it seems that money is the main concern in most people's lives. All money can demonstrate is that you have achieved success in one area of your life. Money is important in our success, but in the eyes of some people, money can make them feel superior. Money can give a false sense of security, thinking that we are better than other people. There is an arrogance and a pompous attitude that can come with financial success if you let it. Success takes in more than the realm of finances. For instance, a drug dealer or a drug runner can make more money in one day than most people can make in a week or even in a month. That is true.

What I also know is that the drug dealer or drug runner may cost you 15 to 20 years of your life in prison that they can never get back. Can you put a price on losing your freedom? You might say, when I get out of prison! You can never put a price on the lost years because of foolish and destructive decisions. It is gone forever. You never get those years back. In the worst-case scenario, being caught up in a bad situation can cause you to lose everything, including your life. Eventually, all poor and deceptive behavior will catch up to you. This is the Law of Sowing and Reaping. The laws of sowing and reaping are constant in motion every minute of the day. The conduct in which you live your life will bring back to you the results, either good or bad. It is the law of reciprocity.

Goals, Gifts, and Dreams

Everyone should have goals, gifts, and dreams to achieve something important in life. To be an achiever, you must contribute something good to the community. The two things you need to recognize are the gifts and talents you were born with, and realize that no one in this life is successful without the help of others. Your goals, desires, and dreams will need to be fine-tuned over the years. It is a working process.

Too many people try to work outside their gifts, talents, and abilities, and when they do, life is not as rewarding or satisfying as they thought. My gifts and talents were in the area where I excelled in at the most. During the course of my life, I tried this and I tried that outside my gifts and talents. Outside my profession, all the extra jobs I had and the businesses I started over a period of time were more of a hobby.

I made money, and I learned from them, but it was not as satisfying as I thought. One of my gifts is in the area of budgeting and administration. You need to understand your gifts and talents. When people jump from job to job, it tells me they are not satisfied inside. There is an uneasiness inside you. Even if you stay in the same field of work, you still jump from job to job. You need to be settled and resolve the issues that are causing you to jump around. Jumping from job to job is like a boat trolling the waters, trying to find the right spot to catch fish or lobsters. They may not be aware of what their gifts and talents are. By the time you finish high school, you should know what move you need to make next concerning your profession.

Your talent and desire may be in a trade school. College can help prepare you for your next important role in life. Higher education will give you the basic foundation to get started. You will move from high school or college to the next level, called on-the-job training. Experience comes with years. Your education can not give you the needed 30 years' experience or tackle the different issues you will face. That has to be worked out on the job. On-the-job training is so vital in becoming the best you can be. This is necessary for personal growth.

You Need Ambition

There are some people who do not have any ambitions or goals in their life. They may work at a gas station or a convenience store as a clerk. That is perfectly fine. You may be built differently with higher ambitions and goals. It could be that your ambition may be to find a trade like welding, plumbing, or carpentry. It may fit you better. We differently need those types of trades to be filled in each generation. Some of my experience came through on-the-job training. Over the years, I learned how to do payroll, manage scheduling, solve complaints, keep up with time sheets, and operate a business through experience that took years. The learning experience is priceless.

Every Role

Remember what I said that everyone is needed in the role they serve in. Everyone is important. We should never look down on any job. People may talk about a job and say, well, they're only a cashier or a sanitation worker. Do without those jobs and see how it affects you on the receiving end. An airplane pilot cannot work if the plane they are flying is not being built. How would they take care of the passengers without a steward or stewardess, or fix any issues with the plane without a mechanic? All the pieces fit together. Every individual contributes to the overall well-being of the community. Do you have some idea what you would like to do?

Dress

To be an achiever and to be successful in life, the one thing you must think about is wearing the appropriate attire. You can't dress sloppily with your pants hanging around your butt if you're going for a job interview. You should not wear your pajamas to work or go to the store. How you dress reflects on what kind of person you may be and how people see you.

You need to look appropriate and dress professionally if you are going to a job interview. You're not the only one they are interviewing for the job. Going to a job interview is a contest. Who is the most qualified, and how you dress and present yourself can set you apart in the hiring process. Always show up for the job interview at least 10 to 15 minutes early. It shows initiative.

False Sense of Entitlement

A person who believes they are entitled is a characteristic trait by an individual believing that they are inherently deserving of special treatment, privilege, attention, or rewards without putting in the necessary effort or having earned them. Every job you contend for should always be on qualifications and never entitlement. Entitlement never brings the experience or qualifications needed to do the job right.

Let me say that by the time you are in your mid-twenties, you should be responsible enough to be living on your own. This is why you need to be thinking about a career so you can begin to achieve your goal. In life, you have to earn your way through. You should never have an attitude of being entitled. Having an entitlement attitude comes from a poverty mentality. People with poverty mentally have no goals or dreams to succeed in life. A poverty mentality is an attitude that tells a person in their mind what one doesn't have rather than what one does have. A poverty mentality is an attitude of thought that says, I can't instead of I can. This kind of mentality keeps a person from growing and achieving success in life. Achievements comes through hard effort and being consistent in life.

Poverty Mentality

A poverty mentality is a terrible cycle that can be passed down from generation to generation. A poverty mentality is a type of victim mentality. People with this mindset often feel powerless, blaming external circumstances, the government, or other people for their failures instead of taking responsibility and seeking solutions. A poverty mentality can largely be attributed to environmental situations, particularly prolonged exposure to systemic stressors such as trauma and a lack of resources and opportunities. This can also come from a feeling of no hope. That type of thinking needs to be broken, and you are the one who can break that vicious cycle. Poverty works against you and not for you.

You can rise up and make a difference. It may not be easy. If no one in your family went to college, you can be the first one. If no one in your family graduated from high school, you can be the first. You can be the first one to make a difference in your family. Remember, free is never free. Someone had to pay for it. People who work to buy have a better appreciation of the items than those who are being handed them. Working to buy for yourself gives a person a sense of purpose, hope, and accomplishment. Successful people worked to achieve what they have. If you have some type of disability, you may need to be helped in life, and that is OK.

Power Station

You are like a power station. You have the ability to empower your life to go in any direction to achieve success. You are not an inferior person. You're not a second-rate individual. You are born in this world to achieve. Your life at home may not have been an ideal situation for growth. Never make a disadvantage or disability your crutch. You are a strong enough individual to overcome any childhood adversity you may have gone through.

Look at President Lincoln. He was a self-taught lawyer and became the 16th president of the United States. Dolly Parton grew up in a poor family in rural Appalachia. Oprah Winfrey was born into a poor Mississippi family in 1954. Do not let your disadvantage be your crutch to make excuses. Jim Carrey and Glenn Beck overcame ADHD through hard work. Harriet Tubman, a legendary poet and Civil Rights Activist with epilepsy, is an Inspiration to all Generations. Halle Berry has both Type One Diabetes and hearing loss. You can make it. I am slightly dyslexic with numbers, with a mild case of ADHD. Reading and understanding were a great difficulty for me. I never let that hold me back. You may not want me to be your accountant. You have the capability to do great things. Don't give up on yourself.

Facing The Issues

I know that being a teenager in high school or college, you will face difficult issues. It is in your teenage years that you can determine what kind of future you will have. There are things in the world that will try to break you down. You don't have to conquer the world in one day. You are building your life, and that takes time. You need to find a pace that fits you. What I mean is, don't jump around from job to job or from course to course to search for your place in the work world. It will be revealed to you. Give your future time to sort out serious thoughts. Whatever you do, while you are in school, do not take any courses that do not mean anything just to get by. Focus. There are students who have taken classes that mean absolutely nothing to their future. Be strategic in your planning. Some students have a degree in a certain field, but it means absolutely nothing to their future.

If you're not sure, then seek good advice from a professional counselor to help guide you. This may help in securing your future. Some of the main issues that young people are facing today are the rampant pace of drugs coming into our country. Keep this in mind, street drugs kill, and it does not care whose life it takes, so don't become a statistic.

Handling Setbacks

An achiever also understands that from time to time, there will be disappointments and setbacks in life. A setback is not a failure. A setback in life may be the opportunity to go in a different direction than the one intended for you. Failure is when you give up on life, and you are not that person. There will always be setbacks. Always remind yourself that when one door closes, another open door is not far from you. When a setback in life takes you by surprise, the achiever begins to meditate on the next move they will make.

Never have a knee-jerk reaction to any setback. Never make quick decisions when you are under enormous pressure. Take a step back and a deep breath. Quitting is not an option. Yes, it may be a little tough to find a new direction. You are built for challenge. This is where your character will grow. Be patient. When you are in a pressured situation to make a knee-jerk decision, always back off. Dealerships and car salespeople are notorious for putting pressure on you to buy that day. You have to give yourself time to think through every decision. The only person who is going to care about you or your budget is YOU.

Being Smart

To be successful in life, a person takes the time to think about consequences and not place themselves in personal jeopardy. They place themselves in a position to solve self-problems before they arise. You also have to give yourself time to think through to find solutions. Never come to the table with a problem without thinking through a solution. At times, you may need to seek some professional advice to help solve personal issues. There is no shame in seeking counsel. Most people, when making a decision, never think through to the consequences or the poor results of their decision.

For instance, when it comes to drinking and driving, which is a very poor decision, because so many unexpected things can go wrong on so many levels. I remember when I was 18 years old, I was coming back from a pizza place. At that time, I could drink what was called 3.2 beers with my friends. My friends and I ordered several pitchers of beer. After a couple of pictures, I was feeling pretty loopy. I did not live too far from the restaurant.

It was around 12:00 at night. There was not much traffic on the road. I told myself, Hey, I just had a few beers. I never counted how many. Time seemed to slip away. Most drinkers don't keep up with the time. As I was coming down Melrose Dr., a startling thought came to me. What if I got pulled over by the police? It was too late now; I was already on the road. The thought suddenly shocked me. I was legally intoxicated, and I knew it even though I could still drive the car. Fortunately, I made it home without any issues. Let me ask you the question to see what your answer would be to me. Was it a smart move to drive that night? I never considered the consequences and what I would lose if I got pulled over.

Be honest. Think about how that one seemingly innocent indiscretion could have affected my life dearly. What if it were you? Would you even think about what you would lose? What would have been the outcome if I or you or I were pulled over by the police? How would it have affected my or your future? We have all done dumb things without thinking about the consequences. There are many loved ones in cemeteries, a wheelchair, or jail because they did not think about the consequences.

All it takes is one wrong decision to damage and exchange your promising future for a life of regret. Being dumb in your decisions can set you back years or even a lifetime. Making a wrong decision can even take your life or the lives of others. Think before you act. Life is never in your favor when you drink and drive or do drugs. You are gambling with your life and your future. Is it worth it? There was a friend I knew in high school, and his father owned a well-known business in our city. I used to go to this business to get work done on my car and see my high school friend helping run the business. In time, my friend took over the business.

He was a very friendly person and had the personality to keep the business running. He was in his 40s when he died of an overdose of cocaine. One wrong decision cost him his life. Don't let this be you.

A Good Follower

Achievers look to better their lives and the lives of others. Their work ethic is performed at a higher level. People who are looking to succeed in life never take shortcuts. They are dependable, reliable, and do not mind being good followers. The best leaders learn to be good followers and study what is necessary to achieve.

What are the Nine Qualities of an Achiever?

1. They believe all things are possible if they believe.
2. They believe good work produces good results.
3. They overcome their fear of defeat.
4. They continuously generate the next step.
5. They are motivated people.
6. They do not hesitate when something needs to be done.
7. They are not lazy people.
8. They are punctual.
9. Before making a life-changing decision, they do the research.

Evidence

Let me speak about evidence. Bringing evidence is a way for the courts to either render a conviction or exonerate a person in a trial. The burden of proof is found in the evidence that is presented. When people are looking at you and your qualities, what kind of proof are you presenting? Does the evidence you present prove of your qualities and standards, or prove your inconsistency and instability as a person? Who you are is found in what you present. This evidence will give people the needed information about who you are as an individual. What do I mean? The evidence that I am talking about is something people ignore.

Suppose a CEO of a corporation or company hires you to come to work. They will depend on you. Everything seems good at first. After six months to a year on the job, something changes. Your work performance and interest begin to drop off. You start out a few minutes late to work. Then it is 10 minutes late, then 15 minutes, and so on. Then you call in sick. It is one excuse after another. You get upset over the littlest issues. Supervisors can see your behavior pattern and may confront you. You begin to argue, and you go into a cussing fit.

That type of behavior is called evidence against you. People will start looking at you differently. People can see the pattern of your behavior change. These changes are patterns that can be seen in every type of relationship. You get what I am trying to say. You create your own evidence for promotion or create evidence to get you released from your job. How you present yourself is up to you. Evidence is something you put out there for everyone to see. It resonates in your attitude. What evidence will you create that will follow you everywhere you go?

You change the attitude; you change the evidence. The evidence that is presented in court can either convict a person or set a person free. The evidence you present can either build your reputation or destroy your reputation. Once your reputation is destroyed, you can hardly get it back. It is like the scarlet letters, NGP. No Good Person. That is one reason why businesses want to examine your resumes and make inquiries before you are hired. Resumes are not just about your qualifications; they also look at why you have jumped from job to job. Resumes reveal something about your work performance and not just your qualifications. A resume, in part, is evidence that can get you the phone call for a job interview or the evidence to send your resume to the trash can.

When I owned a franchise, I would look at a resume to hire someone for a position. Some of the resumes that were given to me ended up immediately in the trash can. Looking at their resume, most could not keep a job for one year before they went somewhere else. It showed me something about them that was not positive. Their lack of loyalty. Companies are looking for people to stay and not become job hoppers. Jumping from job to job does not look good for a company to hire you. You look unstable and unreliable in the workforce.

Credit

There are some companies that are now taking into consideration your credit history as part of their references for hiring. Companies do not want to get caught up in the hassle of their employees having to garnish wages. That makes extra work for the company. Your credit score reveals your financial picture. A person needs to keep their debts low and their credit score high. I know it takes a lot for a person to become a good achiever in their finances. In the workplace, a credit report reveals information to employers that they use to assess a candidate's financial responsibility, reliability, and trustworthiness, particularly for roles involving access to money or sensitive data. It creates a negative perception of your reliability and responsibility. It can make you look less qualified. It is all up to you.

Chapter 6

Born with Will Power

When we talk about willpower, you have to associate it with commitment, dedication, and determination. People have different levels of commitment, dedication, and determination. There are some that do not have any commitment, dedication, or determination. Commitment, dedication, and determination are part of willpower that comes from inside a person, which will help build and protect your future. People in their own minds have different definitions of what dedication is and different ideas of what determination and commitment are. In today's world, what will make you stand out from the rest of the crowd is the willpower not to quit when life gets tough. So many people fail to achieve their goals in life because life or work gets a little tough. What defines a person is their willingness to endure difficult moments and demanding times. I am not talking about abuse or being mistreated.

There was a time when I had a very difficult situation with a captain I was working under, and I was thinking about quitting the fire department. Most people think about quitting their job. I was no different. The challenge to stay was very strenuous. The situation was draining my energy. My willingness to stay was wearing down. This captain was very difficult to work under. Before I would make any final decision to leave, I went to HQ and talked to one of the Deputy chiefs working that night. This Deputy Chief had years of experience and had a tremendous insight and understanding of attitudes. In fact, he alone talked me out of quitting. I was so glad he did. I was soon transferred to a different station to finish out my career. It was a much more pleasant atmosphere with captains who saw the job differently.

The rest of my future success depended on my decision that night. After the deputy Chief talked to me, I gained a different perspective and recovered my willpower to stay and continue my duties. In some ways, he saved my future. I can honestly say it was not me. Others had a difficult time with him as well. A few years later, this captain was transferred to headquarters. By this time, I had already been transferred from under his command.

There was one time the fire crew from station one became so fed up with this captain's attitude, the driver and the firefighters went straight to the Assistant Chief. I'm sure it was not a good meeting. My decisions if I had left would have had a major domino effect in my life. Never make a knee-jerk decision because of present circumstances. Think it through. Like me, get some advice. I am glad I did.

Success or Failure

The level of willpower can determine your level of success or failure in life. People who lack of willpower will seldom achieve their goals and dreams. People who lack willpower seemingly indulge in bad and unhealthy behavior, which traps them in their creation. These types of people will never get ahead in life.

Poor decisions, bad behavior, and self-created vices will continue to break down your life and keep you trapped in a vicious cycle. Even when there seems to be no willpower to tap into, you have to come to the conclusion sometime in your life that enough is enough. When you get to the point in your life that you are fed up, then you will get up. Building willpower in your life can be achieved a little at a time. The first thing you may have to do is trade up your friends who are holding you back. Your drinking buddies will never look out for your good or your future. They will bring you down and help you stay down in life.

That is what I had to do. I knew I had no future hanging out with people who would not motivate me to do better. So I traded up. I knew I did not want to leave my future success in their hands. The next thing you may want to do is begin to prioritize your life one step at a time. I will start to eat better and healthier. Ok, that is a start. Then I will begin to plan out what I want to do. Ok, I will plan my career goals. The next step is to celebrate small accomplishments like quitting your drinking, quit your drugs, or quitting smoking because those things will steal your money, your health, and your future. Begin to think better of yourself.

Raising the Bar

Each positive step you take, you are raising the bar of accomplishment in your life. When I was in high school, we had after-school activities. I was part of the chess club. I wasn't very good at first. I got better the more I played. Then I joined the karate club. For me, that was much more fun. I was more athletic. These clubs helped me grow at that time and protected me from any bad influences in school. It began to give me some of the discipline that I extremely needed. I made new and good solid friends. Over time, I had developed the willpower to learn. Over the years, I have still a sponge absorbing information to learn new things.

Forgive Yourself

Another way you can build willpower is to forgive yourself for any past mistakes that you may have made. Just remember that every bad circumstance that you faced in the past may be keeping you from moving ahead in life. You may now be in a trying and difficult situation. Do not let bad situations keep you from the amazing future that is ahead of you. Each day you wake up is a new day. You cannot do anything about your past mistakes and regrets, but you can start now and do something positive about your future. Yesterday is in your rear-view mirror. I have learned from my past mistakes and blunders. You can too.

Encourage Others

Willpower is built when we begin to encourage others to do better in life, as we are encouraged. To keep your willpower strong, you need to continually nurture it. Building willpower comes with mentally feeding yourself on the right type of information. If you are going to reach higher goals in life, begin to read books that will stimulate you. Give more time to study. Being an encourager is about building confidence in others, offering hope, and helping people see their own potential. This is what good leaders and educators do. There are some people, sad to say, who, no matter how much you try to encourage them, may not listen. Just move on from those types of people. They might drain your energy.

Set Realistic Goals

Set realistic goals for your life. Say you want to be in the medical field. You may even want to be a physician. Start off as an EMT with a local rescue squad or fire department in your community. Then continue to study to become a paramedic. At this stage, you will find out if you want to go further up the ladder. Paramedics can bridge over to become a Physician's assistant. Remember, with every promotion will always come more responsibility. Take it seriously. If so, then apply to a university where you can begin your training as a physician. To become a doctor, a physician's assistant, or a nurse can be very difficult work. These methods apply to any field or career you would like to pursue. It is called climbing the ladder of opportunity. Every goal you desire has a beginning.

As we start off in life, all of us have a beginning point in the field, which we may serve in as we set realistic goals and learn more about our confidence and our chosen profession. Your level of confidence will grow, as will your willpower to accomplish and produce more. It can be a little intimidating to begin in life as we seek out a career field. Do not let intimidation stop you.

Self-Doubt

There will be times when you may question your ability to accomplish your goals in life. This is called self-doubt. Most of us have gone through this phase in life. It is not uncommon. Overcoming self-doubt is a process. It is a feeling of uncertainty about one's own competence, abilities, or decisions. All of us have had some type of reservation when we begin to step out into unknown territory. It is a type of fear that can hold you back.

Let me say from experience, fear is mostly an illusion that we create in our own minds. It is like a mirage. We think it's there, when it is just an illusion. You may think, "What if I fail?" The fear of failure is not having trust in what you can accomplish in this life. You were born to accomplish so much in this life. Training will help you overcome any fear and create in you a strong willpower. Spend time with friends, family, or mentors who are encouraging and who believe in your potential.

To build my willpower and confidence, I went to seminars after seminars, class after class. I went to con-ed classes. I went back to school to finish my Bachelor's, Master's, Master's, and Doctorate degrees. This took a lot of work, willpower, and self-determination on my part. There were times I felt that I could not go on. The more training I did, the more I was prepared for my future. I had more willpower and determination. There were times I wanted to quit. It was difficult. Why? I was mostly a C to a C+ student in high school. I did get A's in gym. I never really applied myself. I am dyslexic to some degree. I did not read very well. These conditions helped me shy away from applying myself in high school. I felt intimidated. I did not feel I was smart enough.

So I held myself back by the way I was thinking. I did not have anyone to push me either. That is one reason I quit high school for over a year. If you took a survey while I was in high school, I would have been voted the least likely to succeed in life. All these issues in my life caused me to doubt myself. I was looking at myself as a victim, a loser, and not someone who could win. What turned me around was that I took an inventory of where my life was and where I wanted my life to be in the next few years. My life was not lining up to where I wanted to be, and the desires I wanted to accomplish were not coming together.

I was just limping through my teenage years. I was brought up in a less-than-desirable atmosphere at home. My parents were hard workers, but not much help in motivating me in the right direction. No matter where you live or what household you were brought up in, you can make it. Inside of you are tremendous abilities that need to be brought out. Your life starting out may not be the best, but it is not how you start, it is all about how you finish.

Resist Those Temptations

Willpower is the ability to resist those negative temptations and urges to do those things that do not benefit your life. Life is not a sprint, it's a marathon. Running well at the end of this race is called life. Let me say this again. One poor and hasty decision can cost you years to recover. Set long-term goals for yourself. Then build the willpower to focus on the task ahead and do not become distracted or preoccupied with trivial and unimportant issues. Overall, choose your associates wisely.

Never let anyone talk you into doing something bad or dangerous that can jeopardize your future. Have the willpower to say No and then walk away. Why? Your associates will not be around in your future. Stay honest and stay focused.

It's My Business

A strong willpower and confidence are built over time. You say to yourself, I want to own my own business someday, maybe it's a restaurant, maybe a pest control company, maybe you would like to own a mechanic shop or transportation. This is called setting up your future. Take the restaurant industry. Owning any business is no easy accomplishment. In a restaurant, the short-term goal is to start out as a dishwasher or become a server. This is the beginning of learning the operation of the business. This is called the ground floor or hands-on experience. There is no substitute for experience. There are so many facets to a business that most people have no understanding of what it takes and the long hours that one has to invest. You need to work your way up to an assistance management position.

This will give you more responsibility and insight into the daily operation. A manager of a restaurant has so many responsibilities that people have no idea about their daily duties or what needs to be done every day. Moving up in a business or company will give you a great understanding if you want to go into business for yourself. As you are growing, you are learning. As you are learning, you are growing.

After years of experience, learning, and training, you will decide if you have the commitment and the knowledge to open your own business. Experience is a powerful teacher. You can't short-circuit these steps. Experience brings wisdom and discernment to navigate through difficult situations to make sound decisions. Don't let your zealous appetite for business outrun your common sense. As you are moving up, treat every position as though it were your own business and work to the best of your ability. Make it your own, but be smart.

There was a gentleman I met when I was selling advertising. He worked for a private school in a town not far from me. He had the ambition to start a restaurant in our city. Nothing wrong with his ambition and dream. He already started the transition when I met with him. In our conversation, I asked him if he had ever worked in a restaurant before. With a smile, he said no, this is my first time running a business. In my mind, even at my younger age, so many flags went up. I sold him the advertisement. He had $40,000.00 of his retirement money invested in his dream. Within one year, his business closed, and his investment was gone. He had zeal but no experience in operating a restaurant, and the sweat that it took to get it up off the ground. The average small business failure rates reported by the U.S. Bureau of Labor Statistics are approximately 20% within the first year and around 50% within five years. Please keep this in mind.

Face The Challenge

As you take on and face the challenges in life, your willpower and your confidence will become more natural to you. As you walk through every challenge you face, the idea of being a failure will be ancient history. Then you will become the person who says, I can do it. Then one issue some people have is that they do not pace themselves when they start to move up. Learn not to take on too many projects or too many courses at one time, so you do not become irritable and frustrated. As you grow, so do your abilities. Pace yourself so you do not become overwhelmed or overloaded. Again, let me say, life is not a sprint, it is a marathon. Your life is not built overnight. So pace yourself.

Reciprocate

Reciprocation is a form of responding to someone who has honored you by doing something good for you. A friend may have invited you and paid for your lunch or dinner, or a person may have done something for you that you could not do. They are not looking to receive anything in return. They did it as friends. When you return that kind deed in some form, you are showing the other person that they are valued and respected.

There are some people in life who all they do is get, get, get, and never give. The one thing you need to get when you see these types of people who always get, get, get is to get rid of them. Did you know wealthy people and politicians fall short in giving?

I know there are some people in your life that you have done so much for and they never at any time returned any kind of favors. It seems all they do is take you for granted. That's ok. In my life, I have done many things for people who have not reciprocated. That's Ok. I have done things for people, and they did not know who gave out the kind gesture. I like to do these kinds of things without recognition. One day, I was at a restaurant, and a friend who works there was suffering terribly from a possible migraine. As a former EMT, I began to ask him some questions. That is just me. I was concerned. We came to the conclusion that it was more likely a migraine. OUCH! I asked him if he had anything to take. He said he had taken some Tylenol.

The Tylenol did not seem to be working. Migraines can be somewhat debilitating. I could tell he was in a lot of pain. After talking with him about OTC medication, I got up from my table and did not hesitate to go to the store and get him some over-the-counter migraine medicine and brought it back to him. He told me later that the medicine did help. He was able to get through the day. My reward was to step in and help a friend. Kindness goes a long way.

Universal Law of Giving

The Universal Law of Giving says the more you give without expecting anything in return, the more the law of reciprocation is put in motion, and more will come back to you. The universal law of giving and the law of reciprocation can never work in a person who has a stingy nature. A person with a stingy nature has developed what I call a poverty mentality. We talked about that. This type of person is more likely to be a selfish and self-centered individual. Some people are like parasites. Always looking for someone to do or give something to.

These types of people are unwilling to give or return any of the favors that they have received. They seem to be very unthankful, with no gratitude. This kind of behavior, I see coming out of an impoverished mind. It may not be all their fault. They may not have any understanding of how the universal law of giving works. The environment they had been raised in may have caused this type of dysfunction. It does not have to be permanent.

They may unknowingly oppose the universal law of giving. The three basic and separate areas of giving are your time, your talent, and your finances. Time and talent can go pretty much hand in hand. If you are a carpenter, plumber, or have a special skill set, and let's say an elderly person or senior citizen may need your services for a small job, and they do not have the funds to cover all or maybe none of the expenses for labor or materials. What would you do?

This is where you can step in to help. I know you can't do this kind of help for everyone. No one expects that. There are occasions when you can step in and help. If you give your time, the law says, more time will be given back to you as though you never missed it. If you give your talent, it will be returned in some area of your life when you need something done that you cannot do. If you give your finances, it will be returned in a greater portion. This is a part of the Law of Reciprocating. That particular person may not be in a position to return the favor, but the universal law of giving and reciprocating is still in motion. You will get it back. Why is this law so important? The universal law has the ability to break poverty in someone's life. It is always better to give than to receive. It's like being a farmer planting seeds for their future harvest.

Poverty itself is being in a constant state of lack, being inferior in one's standard of living, and it will always bring a person into a state of deficiency. In other words, you just don't have enough. The law of giving tells us to guard the honor of the poor and needy. I wish this were an ideal world, but it is not. I know that there are some who will always take advantage of certain situations. Hopefully, they can be weeded out. Don't let the poor conduct of some keep you from helping those who really need it.

Being Challenged

When is giving enough? I know that giving at times can be a mental struggle. Any time we have an opportunity to do good toward someone else, we should. I know that unexpected bills can pop up, or you may be charged more at a repair shop than you thought. You need a refrigerator or tires for your car. You may need to pay back a student loan. I get it. You can still find a way to help give. Let me reiterate, life in general is a marathon, not a sprint. Learning to give is a marathon as well. Early in my giving, I was challenged as well. I always found a way to give, even though it was a sacrifice. I was at one time living from paycheck to paycheck. When I saw the value of The Law of giving, I no longer lived from paycheck to paycheck. I began to witness the universal law of giving begin to work in my life. It is still working today. Let that universal law of giving work for you.

Chapter 7
Born to Learn

Awareness:

"The goal is to promote, encourage, and focus on making the needed resources and support available."

When we are born, we are not aware of our environment around us. I hardly remember my early birthdays. I saw my baby pictures that my parents took, which told me I celebrated my early birthdays. All babies are new to this world. From the time you are born, you begin to absorb information even though you may not consciously process or understand it. Computers are designed like our minds. They are programmed to receive information. Your brain is constantly receiving information. From the time you were conceived in your mother's womb, you began to grow physically. I weighed 6 lbs+ when I was born. As I grew, I got heavier in weight as I ate.

Your birth can be compared with knowledge. Scientists have discovered that while in the womb, babies begin learning language from their mothers. Babies born only hours old are able to differentiate between sounds from their native language and a foreign language and can recognize their mother's voice, especially by the late stages of pregnancy. Your formative years are when a baby's personality is developed over a time period between birth and eight years of age. This is when the brain and neurobiological development are the fastest. During the early stages of childhood, a child's life is when they learn more quickly than at any other time in their development. These are the years in which a child rapidly experiences cognitive (intellectual), social, emotional, and physical development. While in the womb, babies begin learning language from their mother. https://www.washington.edu › news › 2013/01/02

https://www.parentingstyles.com/child-development/formative-years/#:~:text=The%20formative%20years%20are%20the,development%2C%20and%20success%20in%20life.

By the time you enter preschool and kindergarten, your understanding of your environment is becoming more aware to you. As you were growing older, you were becoming more aware of your surroundings. Your foundation for learning was being established. By the time you reach your teenage years, you have absorbed a tremendous amount of information. Some negative information you received may have led you to be somewhat dysfunctional in your behavior. You also absorb good information that can help you make good decisions. As a child, you never had the ability to process, evaluate, or change bad behavior towards you. As a child, you were defenseless against poor and harmful conduct towards you. Your formative years continued to mold your personality into the person you are. When I took Child psychology in college, and came from somewhat of a dysfunctional family situation, I learned a lot about myself and why I felt the way I did. You can't change what you do not know.

I began to identify and deal with some of my dysfunctions. You can too. Sometimes I would listen to other people who saw what I could not.

Your Brain

Your brain is designed to receive information called learning. Your brain needs to learn. Throughout your school years, you were taught a lot of different subjects and received a lot of information. Isn't it amazing how you have the ability to learn all that information? As you process that information, called meditation and study, you have the ability to recall. I know that everyone learns at different levels.

Some are slower learners, and some can learn faster and can retain that information the first time. It was more difficult for me, and it might be for you, too. Don't give up on learning. Keep at it. The realm of knowledge can give you discernment when talking with people. You can become more of a specialist in certain areas. People will learn to trust you if you know what you're talking about. People who do not know and do not want to learn can be easily manipulated in their thinking by false narratives. We see that false narratives are being reported all the time in the media. Learning good and truthful information will keep one from falling for fabrications, lies, and deceit.

Stimulation

All throughout your life, your brain needs to be challenged. You do this through constant learning. When I was growing up, I had a strong desire to play baseball. I played Little League and still play in the senior league today, at least for a few more years. Baseball was my interest. The team that interested me was the N.Y. Yankees, since I lived 30 miles from the stadium. I studied all the information on each player and studied the players' baseball cards. Since then, I have found other things to stimulate my interest, such as the civil war events, ancient history, and counseling. No matter what field or position you are in, finding things to stimulate your mind is very important. Studies show that people who do mentally stimulating activities may have a lower risk of cognitive decline and dementia. This is the case for people who do the activities in both middle age and later life. This is not a remedy for dementia, but it may aid in slowing down the process.

What Do We Need to Do

To stimulate your brain, begin to do things you ordinarily would not do. I have found that not only thinking about your goals and dreams, but writing down your goals is a great way to stimulate your brain. Do it as a reminder. Keep looking at it often. If you have a dream or an idea you want to see fulfilled, keep it in front of you mentally. All ideas and dreams will take time to develop and blossom. Always plan it out. This keeps the dream and ideas alive within you.

There are people who get ahead of the timing of their ideas and feel they have to begin right away. Everything has an appointed time. Dreams and ideas come with proper timing and strategic planning. There have been many successful people who have written their ideas and dreams down on a simple paper napkin at a restaurant. When an idea comes to you, write it down. Dreams and ideas have to come alive in you before they can be seen and witnessed by others. You may want to keep your ideas to yourself for a time. Don't let your passion for the dream out run your common sense. The first lesson, when an idea comes to you, is to count the cost. This book was from an idea, a desire, and planning, and now you're reading it. This was one way I kept stimulating my mind.

Knowing Your Environment

Do you know where everything is in your home or apartment? You say, of course, I do, silly! You want to stimulate your mind? Walk around your house with your eyes blindfolded. Start from a wall and try to walk to the kitchen or the upstairs bathroom very slowly, and see if you can reconstruct your living space in your mind. There are two reasons to do this. Once you are stimulating your mind, in your mind, you are making an outline of your living space, and then, second, if you are caught in a fire or caught in a smoke-filled room, you will know where the doors and windows are. Always be aware of your surroundings. That is how I was trained as a police officer and a member of the ERT unit, now known as S.W.A.T.

You may want to reconstruct the living area by crawling on your knees when blindfolded. That is how we were trained in the fire department. It will not take long. When you're at work or school, know where the exits are in case of an emergency. Know your surroundings. If you are working or going to night school, be sure you protect yourself when walking to your car. Park as close as you can to your destination. Always walk in pairs if possible. Be aware of your surroundings. If you feel uncomfortable, find a security guard or an employee to walk with you. There is safety in numbers.

Activity Is Important

The more your brain is thinking and challenged, the better your memory is likely to be. The wider range of topics you come in contact with will be easier to recall. Join a gym. Exercise contributes to your confidence and is good for your mental health. It increases the circulation of the blood, which will provide more nutrients and oxygen to the brain and throughout the body. Exercise will also help prevent depression, anxiety, and other forms of emotional suffering.

A healthy diet will always benefit your brain and nervous system. So many people's lives are so busy that they eat on the run. We have become, for the most part, junk food junkies. Junk food, over a period of time, decreases our mental ability.

It will make you tired and sluggish and hinder your thoughts. Remembering will become more difficult. If you can build your diet with leafy vegetables and fruits, it will help you tremendously, especially during exams. Believe me, I had to learn to eat broccoli. Still not my favorite food.

You may want to do a crossword puzzle or do some math problems without a calculator to stimulate your mind. If you can sing, join a choir. These things I mentioned will also help with your concentration. Keeping yourself mentally alert as well as physically conditioned. This will make you feel on top of your game and enhance your brain's potential. It will also give you the confidence you may have been lacking.

www.ingramcontent.com/pod-product-compliance
Lightning Source LLC
Chambersburg PA
CBHW040802090726
47818CB00067B/220